COUNTRY

Formal Name: Romania.

Short Form: Romania.

Term for Citizen(s): Romanian(s).

Capital: Bucharest (Bucureşti).

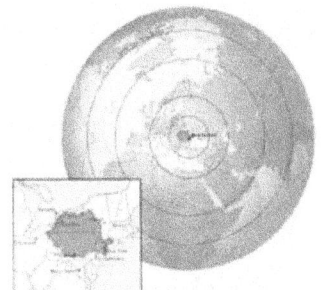
Click to Enlarge Image

Major Cities: As of 2003, Bucharest is the largest city in Romania, with 1.93 million inhabitants. Other major cities, in order of population, are Iaşi (313,444), Constanţa (309,965), Timişoara (308,019), Craiova (300,843), Galati (300,211), Cluj-Napoca (294,906), Braşov (286,371), and Ploeşti (236,724).

Independence: July 13, 1878, from the Ottoman Empire; kingdom proclaimed March 26, 1881; Romanian People's Republic proclaimed April 13, 1948.

Public Holidays: Romania observes the following public holidays: New Year's Day (January 1), Epiphany (January 6), Orthodox Easter (a variable date in April or early May), Labor Day (May 1), Unification Day (December 1), and National Day and Christmas (December 25).

Flag: The Romanian flag has three equal vertical stripes of blue (left), yellow, and red.

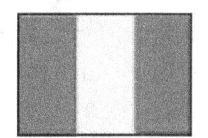
Click to Enlarge Image

HISTORICAL BACKGROUND

Early Human Settlement: Human settlement first occurred in the lands that now constitute Romania during the Pleistocene Epoch, which began about 600,000 years ago. About 5500 B.C. the region was inhabited by Indo-European people, who in turn gave way to Thracian tribes. Today's Romanians are in part descended from the Getae, a Thracian tribe that lived north of the Danube River. During the Bronze Age (about 2200 to 1200 B.C.), these Thraco-Getian tribes engaged in agriculture, stock raising, and trade with inhabitants of the Aegean Sea coast. As trading relations grew with Greek colonies on the western shore of the Black Sea, Greek culture made inroads in the Thraco-Getian settlements. After withstanding invasions by the Scythians, the Persians, and the Macedonians under Alexander the Great, by about 300 B.C. the Getae had forged a state along the lower Danube. From 112 to 109 B.C., the Getae joined Celts who had settled in their state in invading Roman territory in the western Balkans. In the ensuing decades, Roman influence in the region grew as punitive Roman campaigns sought to limit Getian interference in Roman affairs.

After Trajan became Roman emperor in A.D. 98, he launched campaigns to seize control of Getian territory. In A.D. 105 Roman legions captured the Getian capital, Sarmizegetusa (present-day Grădiştea Muncelului). Trajan organized the newly conquered land as the province of Dacia. During the next 200 years, a Dacian ethnic group arose as Roman colonists commingled with the Getae and the coastal Greeks. In A.D. 271 the Emperor Aurelian concluded that Dacia could not be defended from an invasion and ordered his army and colonists to withdraw across the Danube. Without Rome's protection, Dacian settlements were exposed to plunder by invading tribes. The Visigoths, Huns, Ostrogoths, Gepids, and Lombards swept through the land from the third to the fifth centuries. The Avars arrived in the sixth century, along with a steady influx of Slavic peasants. Unlike other tribes, the Slavs settled the land and intermarried with the Dacians. In 676 the first Bulgarian Empire, a unified state to the south, absorbed a large portion of ancient Dacia.

Creation of Moldavia and Walachia: In 896 the Magyars, the last of the migrating tribes to establish a state in Europe, settled in the Carpathian Basin northwest of Dacia. A century later, the Magyar (Hungarian) king Stephen I integrated Transylvania, a region corresponding to the central provinces of modern Romania, into his Hungarian kingdom. The Hungarians constructed fortresses, founded a Roman Catholic bishopric, and began proselytizing Transylvania's indigenous people. In 1241 the Mongols invaded Transylvania from the north and east over the Carpathians. When the Mongols withdrew suddenly in 1242, the Hungarian king Béla IV launched a vigorous reconstruction program in the region. After the Árpád Dynasty of Hungary collapsed in 1301, Transylvania became virtually autonomous.

In the thirteenth and fourteenth centuries, Transylvanian émigrés founded two principalities, Walachia to the south of Transylvania along the Danube and Moldavia to the northeast. These regions steadily gained strength in the fourteenth century, a peaceful and prosperous time throughout southeastern Europe, and Walachia freed itself from Hungarian sovereignty in 1380. In 1417 Walachia became a principality of the Ottoman Empire, which was in the process of enveloping southeastern Europe. Although Transylvania eventually became an autonomous principality of the empire in 1541, in the fifteenth century Moldavia and Walachia slid into severe decline, and under Ottoman rule all the regions of modern Romania became isolated from the outside world. A notable rebel against the Ottomans in the fifteenth century was Vlad Ţepeş, who as the ruler of Walachia (1456–62) gained a reputation for cruelty on which the Dracula legend was built. The Moldavian prince Stephen (1457–1504) led campaigns to keep his territory free of Hungarian and Ottoman control. He succeeded against the Hungarians but failed against the Ottomans. Aided by the Ottoman defeat of Catholic Hungary, in the sixteenth century the Protestant Reformation spread among Transylvania's German and Hungarian populations. The government of Transylvania was among the first in Europe to guarantee a limited freedom of religion.

In the late sixteenth century, several regional powers, including the Holy Roman Empire, vied for de facto control of the Ottoman Empire's Romanian territories. In this complex setting, Michael the Brave of Wallachia (r. 1593–1601) briefly unified Walachia, Moldavia, and Transylvania in 1600 before being assassinated. The legend of Michael's success later inspired the Romanian struggle for cultural and political unity. In the mid-seventeenth century, Moldavia and Wallachia engaged in a mutually costly struggle for regional influence under their respective enlightened leaders, Vasile Lupu and Matei Basarab. Transylvania, meanwhile, experienced a short golden age early in the century but then was ruled by a series of weak Hungarian leaders.

The Struggle for Transylvania: In 1683 Jan Sobieski's Polish army crushed an Ottoman army besieging Vienna, and Christian forces soon began to roll back the Turkish occupation of Europe. In 1699 the Ottoman government officially recognized Austria's sovereignty over Transylvania. Under the rule of the Austrian house of Habsburg, Roman Catholics dominated Transylvania's more numerous Protestants. Vienna mounted a campaign to convert Orthodox clergymen to the Uniate Church, which retained Orthodox rituals but accepted key points of Catholic doctrine and papal authority.

By the early 1700s, the Uniate Church had emerged as a seminal force in the rise of Romanian nationalism. Uniate clergymen schooled in Rome and Vienna acquainted the Romanians with Western ideas, wrote histories tracing their Daco-Roman origins, and adapted the Latin alphabet to the Romanian language, in which they published grammars and prayer books. The Romanians' struggle for equality in Transylvania found a formidable advocate in a Uniate bishop, Inocentiu Micu Klein, who from 1729 to 1744 submitted petitions to Vienna on the Romanians' behalf. The overall status of the Romanians did not improve in the eighteenth century, however; they remained subordinate to both Austrians and Hungarians in the empire. Measures taken by Emperor Joseph II (r. 1780–90) to Germanize the empire catalyzed a national awakening among the Romanians and other minority peoples.

In 1848 a wave of revolution passed through Europe, giving Hungary the opportunity to gain control of Transylvania. Unification with Hungary spurred an armed uprising by the Romanian population. In June 1849, however, Nicholas I of Russia heeded an appeal from Emperor Franz Joseph (r. 1848–1916) and sent in troops who extinguished the revolution. Austria then imposed a repressive regime on Hungary and ruled Transylvania directly through a military governor. In this period, dismal conditions caused many Romanians to flee from Transylvania into Walachia and Moldavia.

Russian Influence on Walachia and Moldavia: Throughout the 1700s and early 1800s, Ottoman rule over Walachia and Moldavia had been interrupted by periods of Russian occupation. Although the Peace of Bucharest nominally returned the principalities to the Ottomans in 1812, complete Russian withdrawal occurred only in 1834. The uprising of Transylvania's Romanian peasants during the 1848 European revolutions ignited Romanian national movements in Walachia and Moldavia. In response, Nicolas I invaded Moldavia and Walachia. In 1854 Russia, under pressure from the Turks and Franz Joseph, withdrew entirely from Walachia and Moldavia, enabling the Ottoman Empire to regain control.

Unification of Moldavia, Transylvania, and Walachia: In 1856 a campaign to unite Walachia and Moldavia began, and in 1859 assemblies at Bucharest and Iaşi elected the noble Alexandru Ioan Cuza governor of both principalities. All the powers ratified Cuza's election, and the two principalities officially became Romania in 1861. Cuza's rule was marked first by reform and then by political instability. Cuza was deposed and replaced by the German Carol (Charles) of Hohenzollern-Sigmaringen (r. 1866–1914), who backed Russia during the Russo-Turkish War of 1877–78. After the Ottomans' defeat in that conflict, Carol proclaimed Romania's independence, ending five centuries of vassalage. In 1881 the parliament proclaimed Romania a kingdom, and Carol was crowned in Bucharest. Transylvania and Bessarabia, each with a Romanian majority population, remained part of the Austro-Hungarian Empire and the Russian Empire, respectively.

The Kingdom of Romania enjoyed relative peace and prosperity for the next three decades. Walachian wells began pumping oil, a bridge was built across the Danube at Cernavoda (in Dobruja), and new docks rose at Constanța. Carol equipped a respectable army, and rural schools were built. Romania borrowed heavily to finance such development, however, and most of the population continued to live in poverty. After the outbreak of World War I and the death of Carol, Romania eventually joined the side of Britain, Russia, France, and Italy, declaring war on Austria–Hungary in August 1916 under the leadership of Ferdinand, Carol's nephew and successor (r. 1914–27).

In 1919 Romanians voted in the country's first free elections. Two postwar agreements, the Treaty of Saint-Germain with Austria and the Treaty of Trianon with Hungary, more than doubled Romania's size, adding Transylvania, Dobruja, Bessarabia, northern Bukovina, and part of the Banat region from Serbia. In this way, the treaties fulfilled the centuries-long dream of uniting all Romanians in a single country.

The Interwar Years and World War II: In October 1922, Ferdinand became king of Greater Romania, and in 1923 Romania adopted a new constitution providing for a highly centralized state. In 1924 the government banned the Communist Party of Romania, which had been founded in 1921. Romania's economy boomed during the interwar period, but the international financial crisis that began in 1929 sent world grain prices tumbling and plunged Romania, heavily dependent on grain exports, into an economic tailspin. The downturn provided fertile ground for the formation of the Iron Guard, a political cult consisting of malcontents, unemployed university graduates, thugs, and anti-Semites who called for war against Jews and communists. The Iron Guard soon became the Balkans' largest fascist party. In September 1940, the Iron Guard, with the support of Germany and renegade military officers led by the premier, General Ion Antonescu, forced Ferdinand's successor, Carol II, to abdicate in favor of his 19-year-old son, who became Michael V (r. 1940–47). Antonescu soon usurped Michael's authority and brought Romania into the German camp. In June 1941, Romanian forces supported the attack by German armies on the Soviet Union. During the war, Antonescu's regime severely oppressed the Jews in Romania and the conquered territories. Despite rampant anti-Semitism, however, most Romanian Jews survived the war.

In August 1943, King Michael led a coalition of opposition groups that overthrew the Antonescu government. The coup speeded the Soviet Army's advance westward and ended Romania's war against the Allies. The Soviet Army occupied Bucharest in August 1944. Romania and the Soviet Union signed an armistice that granted the Romanian regions of Bessarabia (eastern Moldavia) and Bukovina, along the border of Ukraine, to the Soviet Union. In October 1944, British Prime Minister Winston Churchill proposed to his Russian counterpart Josef Stalin a list of respective degrees of interest of the Soviet Union and the Western Allies in occupied European countries. Stalin accepted Churchill's offer of 90 percent Soviet preponderance in Romania, foreshadowing Romania's geopolitical position in the postwar era.

The Move Toward Socialism: In late 1944, Romania's Communist Party recruitment campaigns began attracting large numbers of workers, intellectuals, and others disillusioned by the breakdown of the country's democratic experiment. In 1945 the Soviet-backed Romanian Communist Party seized power, and in 1947 King Michael abdicated under pressure from the Communists. In June 1948, the national assembly enacted legislation nationalizing the country's banks and most of its industrial, mining, transportation, and insurance companies. Within three years, the state controlled 90 percent of Romania's industry. In January 1949, Romania joined the Council for Mutual Economic Assistance (Comecon), the Soviet-dominated economic federation of East European and other communist countries. Forced agricultural collectivization was initiated to feed the growing urban population, and an ambitious program of forced industrial development was launched at the expense of agriculture and consumer-goods production. Fast-paced industrialization soon began reshaping the country's social fabric as peasants left their villages for factory jobs in urban areas.

The early years of Communist Party rule saw a bitter power struggle. After Stalin's death in March 1953, Prime Minister Gheorghe Gheorghiu-Dej was able to establish a unified party leadership supported by a loyal internal apparatus. Gheorghiu-Dej forged a "New Course" for Romania's economy and set Romania on a so-called "independent" course within the Eastern bloc. Although following a Stalinist model of domestic economic development, Gheorghiu-Dej defied Soviet hegemony over the Eastern bloc internationally. He initiated economic and political ties with China and Yugoslavia, both of which had split with the Soviet Union on a number of issues. He also established domestic programs of "de-Russification" and "Romanianization."

The Rise of Nicolae Ceauşescu: After Gheorghiu-Dej's death in March 1965, Nicolae Ceauşescu, the party's first secretary, quickly consolidated power and eliminated rivals. Romania's divergence from Soviet policies widened under Ceauşescu. Popular acceptance of Ceauşescu's regime peaked with his defiance of the Soviet Union's armed response to the "Prague Spring" uprising in Czechoslovakia in 1968; most Romanians believed his actions had averted Soviet re-occupation of their country.

During his early years in power, Ceauşescu presented himself as a reformer and populist champion of the common man. Purge victims began returning home; contacts with the West multiplied; and artists, writers, and scholars found new freedoms. After consolidating power, however, Ceauşescu regressed. The government again disciplined journalists and demanded the allegiance of writers and artists to socialist realism. By the early 1970s, Ceauşescu had adopted the principle of cadre rotation, making the creation of opposition power bases impossible. In 1973 Ceauşescu's wife Elena became a member of the ruling Politburo, and in 1974 voters "elected" Ceauşescu president.

Dynastic Socialism: The Eleventh Communist Party Congress in 1974 signaled the beginning of a regime based on "dynastic socialism." Ceauşescu placed five members of his immediate family in control of defense, internal affairs, planning, science and technology, youth, and party cadres. Ceauşescu launched monumental, high-risk ventures, including huge steel and petrochemical plants, and he restarted work on the Danube–Black Sea Canal, which had been halted for 23 years. Central economic controls tightened, and imports of foreign technology skyrocketed.

Halfway through the Sixth Five-Year Plan (1976–80), the economy faltered. A devastating earthquake, drought, higher world interest rates, declining foreign demand for Romanian goods, and higher prices for petroleum imports pushed Romania into a balance-of-payments crisis. Ceauşescu imposed a crash program to pay off the foreign debt. The government cut imports, slashed domestic electricity usage, and squeezed its farms, factories, and refineries for exports. Ceauşescu's debt-reduction policies caused average Romanians terrible hardship.

By the mid-1980s, Romania's economy was increasingly dependent on the Soviet Union for energy imports and raw materials, and as a noncompetitive market for Romanian goods. Despite this dependence, in the late 1980s Ceauşescu was vocal in his criticisms of the liberalization policies of General Secretary Mikhail Gorbachev in the Soviet Union. In 1989 Ceauşescu was reelected for another five-year term as general secretary of the Romanian Communist Party.

The Fall: In 1989, as communist governments fell peacefully throughout the Eastern bloc states from the Baltic Sea to the Balkans, Ceauşescu maintained his iron grip on Romania. It seemed for a time that the regime liberalization taking place elsewhere might bypass Romania entirely. When cracks finally appeared in the regime, however, Ceauşescu's decline from power was swift and violent. In December 1989, protesters in Timişoara filled the streets after government efforts to remove a pastor from his church. Eventually, the crowd called for the end of Ceauşescu's regime. On December 17, Ceauşescu ordered the minister of national defense to fire on the crowd in order to end the demonstrations. Gunfire by Securitate (secret police) forces killed and wounded scores of demonstrators.

Foreign radio broadcasts spread word of the Timişoara uprising to the rest of the country, and protests began in Bucharest. At a televised pro-regime rally the next day, Ceauşescu's address to a large crowd of supporters was interrupted by chants of revolutionary slogans. Dumbfounded, the aged ruler yielded the microphone, and the once unassailable Ceauşescu regime suddenly appeared vulnerable.

After a second unsuccessful attempt to address a crowd and news that the army was joining the protesters, Ceauşescu and his wife fled the capital but were captured several hours later. In the days that followed, confused battles among military and Securitate factions raged in the streets. The media's grossly exaggerated casualty figures convinced citizens that Romania faced a protracted, bloody civil war. Against this ominous backdrop, a hastily convened military tribunal tried Nicolae and Elena Ceauşescu for "crimes against the people," and their death sentences were carried out on Christmas Day. A jubilant Romania celebrated news of the executions.

Post-Ceauşescu Romania: Political and economic stability has not come easily to Romania since the fall of the Ceauşescu regime. Until the early 2000s, one party, which began as the National Salvation Front (NSF), dominated Romanian politics under a variety of names. In what was essentially a palace coup, Ion Iliescu, a former member of the party elite, seized power after the execution of the Ceauşescus. Iliescu quickly repealed many of Ceauşescu's most unpopular policies, paving the way for victory by the center-left NSF in the 1990 elections. The NSF faced serious social, political, and economic concerns that it was ill equipped to address effectively. Corruption was rampant, and many feared that Iliescu and his allies lacked a sincere commitment to democracy. Pro-democracy protests in Bucharest in 1990 were suppressed violently by miners from the Jiu Valley, who many believed were directed by Iliescu. In 1991 the miners made a second violent return to Bucharest, this time to protest market reforms advocated by Prime Minister Petre Roman, a rival of Iliescu. The government collapsed, the NSF split into two factions, and elections were held in 1992.

The 1992 elections returned Iliescu and his branch of the NSF (now called the Democratic National Salvation Front, or FDSN) to power. Significant reform did not take place under Iliescu's leadership. In 1993 the FDSN renamed itself the Party of Social Democracy in Romania (PSDR). In 1996 Iliescu lost a presidential runoff to the academician Emil Constantinescu, who led an unstable center-right alliance. Living standards declined in the late 1990s, weakening support for Constantinescu. In the 2000 elections, voters once again put their faith in the well-known Iliescu, who won a runoff with Corneliu Vadim Tudor, leader of the extreme nationalist Greater Romania Party. After the elections, the PSDR was renamed yet again, this time as the Social Democratic Party (PSD). The PSD then presided over a period of relative stability as living standards rebounded somewhat. However, in the 2004 presidential election Bucharest mayor Traian Basescu, leader of a center-right coalition, unexpectedly defeated the PSD, and a coalition including the Democratic Party and the National Liberal Party formed a government.

In April 2005, Bulgaria and Romania signed an accession treaty with the European Union (EU), calling for admission to that organization in 2007 or 2008. For Romania this would be the second major step in forging ties with Western Europe; in 2004 it achieved membership in the North Atlantic Treaty Alliance (NATO). In December 2005, U.S. Secretary of State Condoleeza Rice signed an agreement for the permanent stationing of U.S. troops in Romania, the first such treaty by the United States with a former Warsaw Pact country. In September 2006, the European Commission, the EU's administrative and legal arm, recommended the admission of Bulgaria and Romania in January 2007, with the requirement that those countries make substantial reforms to gain permanent status. In late 2006, a change of Romania's government, a breakup of the four-party coalition elected in 2004, and early elections (2007 instead of 2008) were under discussion for the period following EU accession.

GEOGRAPHY

Location: Romania is located in southeastern Europe. Ukraine lies to the north and east, Moldova to the northeast, Hungary to the northwest, Serbia to the southwest, Bulgaria to the south, and the Black Sea to the southeast.

Size: Romania's total area is 237,500 square kilometers, 7,160 square kilometers of which is water.

Click to Enlarge Image

Land Boundaries: Romania shares land boundaries with the following nations: Bulgaria (608 kilometers), Hungary (443 kilometers), Moldova (450 kilometers), Serbia (476 kilometers), and Ukraine (431 kilometers).

Disputed Territory: Romania and Ukraine continue to negotiate conflicting claims to the Ukrainian-administered Snake Island (Simony Island in Ukrainian, Insula Serpilor in Romanian) offshore from the Danube Delta, as well as their common Black Sea maritime boundary.

Length of Coastline: Romania's coastline along the Black Sea is 225 kilometers long.

Maritime Claims: Romania claims a territorial sea of 12 nautical miles, a contiguous zone of 24 nautical miles, an exclusive economic zone of 200 nautical miles, and a continental shelf of 200 meters (or to the depth of exploitation).

Topography: Romania's topography is almost evenly divided among mountains, hills, and plains. These varied forms spread rather symmetrically from the Carpathian Mountains, which reach elevations of more than 2,500 meters in central Romania, to the Danube Delta in the southeast, which is a few meters above sea level. After running from northwest to southeast from the border of Ukraine, the southern expanse of the Carpathians, known as the Transylvanian Alps, forms a loop and runs from east to west, crossing the Danube in the Iron Gate region. A lesser mountain range, the Bihor Massif, is located in northwestern Romania. Because of the relatively modest elevations of the mountains and the existence of passes, the Carpathians have not posed a serious obstacle to transportation across the country. Within the loop of the Carpathians is the Transylvanian Plateau, the largest tableland in Romania and an important agricultural region. South of the Carpathians, an extensive plain stretches northward from the Danube and occupies most of southeastern Romania.

Principal Rivers: The Danube is Romania's major waterway. After entering the country in the southwest at Bazias, the Danube travels some 1,000 kilometers through or along Romanian territory, forming the southern frontier with Serbia and Bulgaria. One of Europe's largest hydroelectric stations is located at the Iron Gate, where the Danube surges through the Carpathian gorges on the Serbian border. Virtually all of the country's rivers are tributaries of the Danube, either directly or indirectly, and by the time the Danube's course ends in the Black Sea, these waterways account for nearly 40 percent of the total discharge. The most important of the Danube tributaries in Romania are the Mures, Olt, Prut, Siret, Ialomita, Somes, and Arge. Romania's rivers flow primarily east, west, and south from the central crown of the Carpathians. They are fed by rainfall and melting snow, which causes considerable fluctuation in volume and occasionally catastrophic flooding.

Climate: Because of its position in the southeastern portion of the European continent, Romania has a climate that is transitional between temperate and continental. In the extreme southeast, Mediterranean influences offer a milder, maritime climate. The average annual temperature is 11° C in the south and 8° C in the north. In Bucharest the temperature ranges from –29° C in January to 29° C in July, with average temperatures of –3° C in January and 23° C in July. Rainfall, although adequate throughout the country, decreases from west to east and from mountains to plains. Some mountainous areas receive more than 1,000 millimeters of precipitation each year.

Natural Resources: Romania possesses modest and declining reserves of petroleum and natural gas in addition to timber, coal, iron ore, and salt, as well as arable land and hydropower resources.

Land Use: According to the Romanian government, arable areas represent 39.5 percent of land; forests, 28 percent; pastures and hayfields, 20.5 percent; vineyards and orchards, 2.3 percent; buildings, roads, and railroads, 4.5 percent; water and ponds, 3.7 percent; and other areas, 1.8 percent.

Environmental Factors: Romania's past focus on heavy industry has saddled it with a legacy of industrial pollution, and pollution presents a serious threat to Romania's environment. Under Ceauşescu, Romania's Environmental Law of 1973 was never fully enforced. When the Law on Environmental Protection finally updated national environmental regulations in 1995, Romania was one of the last countries in Eastern Europe to do so. According to Western observers, toxic air emissions present the most significant environmental hazard in Romania. Industrial waste pollution in waterways is also significant. In January 2000, a major cyanide spill in Romania's mining region flooded the Danube River with toxic waste; the contamination killed fish and polluted drinking water in Romania, Hungary, Serbia, and Bulgaria before dissipating in the Black Sea. Approximately 18 percent of Romania's water is too polluted even for industrial use. Economic difficulties and political constraints have prevented widespread reform of heavy industry, especially mining, and kept environmental protections generally weak. However, beginning in 2004 impending membership in the European Union (EU) has stimulated substantial upgrading of environmental monitoring and legislation in order to comply with EU standards by 2007. In 2006 the European Commission listed Romania's two main remaining issues as increased transparency of environmental decisions and improved waste management. Romania has received extra time to reach full compliance on environmental matters. The agency responsible for environmental protection is the Ministry of Water Resources, Forests, and Environmental Protection, which has an office in each of the 41 counties.

Time Zone: Romania is two hours ahead of Greenwich Mean Time.

SOCIETY

Population: Romania's population has declined every year since 1990 as a result of falling birthrates, increasing mortality rates, and emigration. In 2006 Romania's population was estimated at 22.3 million, with an annual growth rate of –0.1 percent. In 2005 some 66 individuals were granted asylum in Romania, and 450 Uzbek refugees received temporary asylum pending resettlement elsewhere. In 2006 the estimated net migration rate was –0.13 per 1,000 population. Estimates of the number of Romanians who have emigrated since 1989 range from 600,000 to 2 million. Population density in Romania in 2006 was 93.9 persons per square kilometer. Slightly more than half of the population lives in urban areas.

Demography: In 2006 some 15.7 percent of the population was less than 15 years of age, and those aged 65 and older accounted for 14.7 percent of the population. In the overall population, there were 0.95 males for every female. The number of births per 1,000 was 10.7, the number of deaths, 11.8. The infant mortality rate per 1,000 live births was 25.5, one of the highest rates in Europe. The maternal mortality rate, 49 per 100,000 live births in 2000, was six times the rates in Hungary and Poland in 2005. In 2006 the fertility rate was 1.37 children born per woman. Life expectancy at birth was estimated at 71.6 years (68.1 years for men, 75.3 years for women), among the lowest averages in Europe.

Ethnic Groups: The majority of the population (89 percent) is ethnic Romanian, with a small minority of Hungarians (7.1 percent). Roma officially account for 2.5 percent of the population, but their actual share is believed to be substantially higher. Nationalities with smaller populations are Croats, Germans, Russians, Serbs, Turks, and Ukrainians.

Languages: Romanian is the official language. Hungarian is commonly used as well, particularly in the western and northwestern areas. English and French are widely spoken as second and third languages, especially among younger Romanians.

Religion: According to the Romanian government, 86. 7 percent of the population was Eastern Orthodox, 4.7 percent Roman Catholic, 3.2 percent Protestant, less than 1 percent Greek Catholic, and less than 1 percent Jewish as of 2003.

Education and Literacy: Although the education system has undergone substantial structural changes in the early 2000s, low funding precipitated a major teachers' strike in November 2005. The 2006 budget increased government spending on education to 5 percent of the gross domestic product (GDP), and teacher salaries increased by 12 percent in 2006. However, funding remains very low by European standards, and there is a shortage of qualified teachers. Education was one target of the campaign to decentralize state services that President Basescu began in 2006.

Education in Romania is compulsory for the first 10 years of schooling, beginning at age six. In 2003 some 96.5 percent of eligible children attended the primary school grades, and 77 percent attended kindergarten. Following primary school, several types of education are available: general secondary schools, which require an entrance exam and prepare students for college-level studies; specialized secondary schools, which offer agricultural, industrial, and teacher training; art schools; and vocational schools. The average dropout rate following the compulsory years is about 25 percent, but the rate is much higher in poor areas and among the Roma population. In 2004 Romania had about 10,400 primary and secondary schools attended by 3.2 million students and staffed by 216,000 teachers. After substantial increases in the early 2000s, by 2005 Romania's institutions of higher education had about 650,000 students, one-quarter of whom were in private institutions. In 2003 the literacy rate in Romania was 98.4 percent (99.1 percent male, 97.7 percent female).

Health: Health care is generally poor by European standards, and access is limited in many rural areas. In 2001 health expenditures were equal to 6.5 percent of gross domestic product. In 2005 there were 1.9 physicians and 7.4 hospital beds per 1,000 people. The state-owned health care system was a target of the campaign to decentralize state services that President Basescu began in 2006. The system has been funded by the National Health Care Insurance Fund, to which employers and employees make mandatory contributions. Private health insurance has developed slowly. Because of low public funding, about 36 percent of the population's health care spending is out-of-pocket. Bribes frequently are paid to gain improved treatment.

The most common causes of death are cardiovascular disease and cancer. Communicable diseases such as tuberculosis, syphilis, and viral hepatitis are more common than elsewhere in Europe. The incidence of human immunodeficiency virus/acquired immune deficiency syndrome (HIV/AIDS) has been less than 0.1 percent. However, high rates of venereal disease, lack of education about HIV prevention, and increasing intravenous drug use are factors that could increase the rate substantially in the future. The number of pediatric AIDS cases is one of the highest in Europe because of unsafe blood transfusion and inoculation procedures for young children in hospitals and clinics in the last years of the communist era. In 2006 an estimated 7,200 Romanians below age 20 had been infected in this way.

Welfare: In 2005 some 22 percent of Romanians, including about 80 percent of Roma, lived below the poverty line. The northeastern region had the highest poverty rate, Bucharest the lowest. The Romanian social insurance system, which underwent major reform in 2000, is funded by employee/employer contributions and government payments. The system provides a variety of benefits, including old-age pensions, disability benefits, workers' compensation for injuries sustained on the job, unemployment benefits, and family allowances. The system suffers from a shortage of capital and human resources, as well as poor distribution, especially in rural areas. Workers with sufficient years of contribution can receive pensions at age 57 (women) or 63 (men). In 2015 the minimum age will be 65 for both sexes, and minimum years of contribution will increase. In 2007 supplementary individual social security accounts will be established, with mandatory contributions from workers younger than 35. The child welfare system, a legacy of the Ceauşescu regime, was a chronic problem through the early 2000s. After a failed effort in 2002 to modernize child welfare law to meet European Union standards, a new law substantially improved the system in 2005. The number of children abandoned at hospitals decreased by 50 percent between 2003 and 2005.

ECONOMY

Overview: The pace of Romania's transition from a centrally planned to a market economy has been slower than in neighboring postcommunist states. Following the 1989 revolution, governments enacted economic reforms sporadically. During the 1990s, macroeconomic imbalances persisted, as did government subsidies for loss-making industries. Fiscal debt and inflation were problems throughout the decade. Although the multinational agencies that financed many of Romania's economic growth programs exerted pressure to pursue stabilization and restructuring programs, Romania failed to fulfill the terms of any of the standby agreements it had with the International Monetary Fund in the 1990s. The governments since 2001 have exercised significantly more financial discipline. With membership in the European Union (EU) in 2007 as an incentive, measures such as a flat income tax, a revised labor code, a revised capital account policy, and stronger anti-inflationary efforts have solidified many aspects of Romania's economy. Privatization has been slow and uneven; in 2005 more than 1,000 enterprises still were state-owned. In 2004 the EU's European Commission declared that Romania has a functioning market economy, although in 2005 the commission still identified significant deficiencies. Although by 2006 Romania had resolved enough deficiencies to receive final approval for EU membership in January 2007, recent economic growth has not yet alleviated Romania's widespread poverty, and corruption and bureaucracy continue to hinder business activities.

Gross Domestic Product (GDP): In the wake of the Ceauşescu regime, which sacrificed overall economic growth in order to eliminate the country's foreign debt, Romania's GDP still was increasing slowly in the early 2000s. In 2003 the GDP was still below the 1989 level. A new government economic policy, including significant tax reform and privatization, caused the GDP to increase by 4.5 percent in 2005 to US$72.5 billion. The predicted figure for 2006 was US$77.6 billion (an increase of 7 percent over 2005) or US$3,480 per capita. In 2004 agriculture contributed 10.1 percent of GDP, industry 35 percent, and services, 54.9 percent. The private-sector share was 70 percent.

Government Budget: Although budget deficits have declined since 1999, in most years government expenditures have exceeded revenues. The 2004 budget showed a deficit of US$800 million, based on revenues of US$21.7 billion and expenditures of US$22.5 billion. In 2005, the first year of Romania's new flat income tax, expenditures were US$31.4 billion and revenues, US$30 million, yielding a deficit of US$1.4 billion. The draft budget for 2007 includes US$48.7 billion in revenues and US$51.4 billion in expenditures, a deficit of US$2.7 billion.

Inflation: For most of the postcommunist period, Romanians endured double- and even triple-digit inflation. Inflation in this period peaked in 1993 at 256 percent. After reaching another alarmingly high rate at 151 percent in 1997, inflation began a steady decline that continued through 2005. From 2001 to 2005, the rate dropped from 34.5 percent to 9 percent. Estimates of the inflation rate for 2006 ranged from 6.1 to 6.4 percent. The official inflation target for 2007 is 4.4 percent. Some outside observers have noted that Romania's consumer price index fails to accurately reflect the true impact of energy costs, which are rising faster than average.

Agriculture: Romania has rich agricultural lands, with conditions amenable to a variety of crops, and has historically been a major agricultural producer. Since 1989, no other industry has been privatized as extensively as agriculture. By 2004 some 85 percent of arable land and 98 percent of livestock were privately held. Nevertheless, the agriculture sector remains weaker than in other new member states of the European Union. Although in 2004 agriculture accounted for more than 30 percent of total employment and 68 percent of rural employment, it contributed only 10 percent of gross domestic product. After the postcommunist redistribution of 80 percent of arable land to private owners in parcels of limited size, by 2000 only 2 percent of farms were larger than 10 hectares. This fragmentation, a result of the original redistribution policy and the slow pace of subsequent consolidation, has contributed to the under-capitalization and under-mechanization of the sector. Legal, financial, and political restrictions continue to stifle growth. Agricultural production for 2005 was reduced by serious floods during the growing season. In order of volume, in 2004 the principal crops included corn, wheat, potatoes, sunflower seeds, barley, tomatoes, grapes, apples, cabbages, and sugar beets; principal livestock inventories included chickens, sheep, pigs, and cattle.

Forestry: In 2000 Romania had about 6.5 million hectares of forest cover. Timber output remained steady in the early 2000s. In 2004, 15,800 cubic meters of timber products were harvested, of which about 3,000 cubic meters were fuelwood.

Fishing: In 2003 the total fish output in Romania was 19,092 tons, almost equally divided between aquaculture and wild harvest. That figure was a significant increase from the 2002 total of 16,237 tons. The output included mainly several species of carp, sprat, and bream.

Mining and Minerals: The mining sector has declined in the postcommunist era, in part as a result of poor maintenance and a lack of investment, and the industry has a poor environmental record. Romania has modest deposits of minerals, including bauxite, brown coal, copper, gold, iron ore, lead, salt, uranium, and zinc. Reserves of bauxite are estimated at 2.5 million tons, copper at 1.5 million tons, zinc at 1.4 million tons, and lead at 600,000 tons. In 2003 salt production totaled 2.4 million tons, unprocessed iron ore 244,000 tons, brown coal 31,000 tons, zinc 23,500 tons, and lead 18,100 tons.

Industry and Manufacturing: The industry and manufacturing sector has been burdened by a preponderance of old, in some cases obsolete, plants in the metallurgical, heavy engineering, and chemical industries. The communist-era practice of concentrating manufacturing facilities left the country with a number of aging, unwieldy industrial enterprises. Restructuring and the closing of inefficient factories initially weakened the sector, but between 2000 and 2004 such measures yielded a 25 percent overall increase in industrial output. Until the early 2000s, privatization progressed at a slower pace than in other sectors of the economy, but beginning in 2001 the pace accelerated, and increased rates of foreign investment made possible large-scale modernization. Major industrial products include textiles, shoes, tires, cement, crude steel, household consumer items, passenger cars, tractors, wine, and beer. In the early 2000s, the fastest-growing industries have been automobiles and pharmaceuticals, both of which have been supported significantly by foreign direct investment. In recent years, major export industries such as textiles and shoes have been hurt by competition from developing countries. Beginning in the early 2000s, the construction industry, which suffered in the economic decline of the 1990s, has benefited from expanded demand for housing, retail outlets, highway construction, and tourist facilities, and this trend is expected to continue.

Energy: Analysts generally agree that Romania is the only Central European country with significant primary energy reserves (both fossil fuel and hydroelectric resources) offering the potential for several decades of energy self-sufficiency. With 6 percent of the Romanian labor force working in the energy sector, it is the third largest employer in the country, accounting for 5 percent of total industrial output. Since 2000, the Romanian government has accelerated efforts to restructure and privatize the inefficient systems of energy production and distribution inherited from the Ceauşescu regime.

Although Romania has substantial reserves of coal, natural gas, and oil, the output of each has declined substantially in the past decade, and the decline is expected to continue. As of 2003, Romania had proven crude oil reserves of about 900 million barrels. That year production averaged 123,000 barrels per day, compared with 294,000 barrels per day in 1976. About 10 percent of crude oil production is from offshore wells in the Black Sea, where further exploration is planned. The output of natural gas, reserves of which are estimated at 300 billion cubic meters, declined by 70 percent between 1982 and 2004. Most of the natural gas consumed in Romania is imported from Russia via the Progress pipeline. Romania's 10 oil refineries and its natural gas extraction company are state-owned; the government sold the principal oil company, Petrom, to an Austrian company in 2004. Proven coal reserves in 2005 were about 1.5 billion tons, mostly lignite and subbituminous. Annual coal production peaked in 1989 at 66.4 million tons but since then has declined by more than 50 percent.

Romania has an installed electricity generating capacity of 22.2 gigawatts, making it the largest power producer in southeastern Europe and a net electricity exporter. Operational capacity, however, is only 16 gigawatts. In 2005 Romania produced 60.1 million megawatt-hours of electricity, 72.9 percent of which came from various types of thermoelectric plants, 17 percent from hydroelectric plants, and 10.1 percent from its one nuclear plant. Recent improvements to the energy infrastructure include rehabilitation of 10 thermal power stations (combined capacity 1.36 gigawatts, completed in 2005), upgrading the transmission network, and constructing a second unit at the Cernavoda nuclear power plant, which is expected to go online in 2007. Cernavoda's one operational unit has an installed capacity of 655 megawatts. Work on a third unit of the Cernavoda station was scheduled to begin in 2006 and reach completion in 2011. Current exploitation of hydropower resources is far below capacity. The U.S. Department of Energy estimates that Romania may have more than 5,000 locations favorable to hydroelectric power plants. In 2004 Romania's hydroelectric plants had 6,007 megawatts of installed capacity.

Services: In 2004 the services sector accounted for 54.9 percent of gross domestic product and services employed 37.7 percent of the labor force. Despite rapid development in the postcommunist era, the services sector remains underdeveloped by Western standards. According to a 2001 assessment by the U.S. Department of Commerce, areas in the services sector expected to register the fastest growth include information and communications technology, banking, financial services, insurance, accounting, tourism, and advertising and other media development.

Privatization and restructuring of banking and financial services began after much delay in December 1998 with the sale of the state's majority stake in the Romanian Development Bank. By 2003 state-owned banks accounted for 40 percent of total net assets, compared with 75 percent in 1998. With the full privatization of the Banca Comerciala Romana, the largest bank in Romania, in 2006 the state's share fell to 7.5 percent. The number of banks has declined, mostly through mergers and the closing of inefficient banks, to 32 in 2006. Of that number, the 23 that were majority foreign-owned accounted for 66 percent of nongovernment lending and 55 percent of total deposits. Practices at domestic banks continue to favor short-term lending at the expense of investment in new ventures and existing small and medium enterprises. Oversight and regulation of the commercial banking system have improved, reducing vulnerability. Rural areas generally lack banking services, hindering the financing of agricultural enterprises.

The Bucharest Stock Exchange (BSE) resumed trading in 1995, and the RASDAQ, an electronic network for registering over-the-counter share sales, was launched the following year. Growth in the BSE composite index grew (in nominal terms) by 26 percent in 2003, 104 percent in 2004, and 38 percent in 2005. The equity market, whose capitalization was US$19.3 billion at the end of 2005, remained relatively small but has received increased foreign investments. Romania's non-bank financial services and insurance sectors remained poorly developed in 2006.

Romania has a variety of natural resources that could serve the tourism industry well, including the Black Sea and Danube Delta regions, the Carpathians and Transylvania, and a well-established wine industry. However, growth in tourism has been hindered by poor infrastructure, in particular a shortage of luxury hotels. Foreign investment in tourism has not been brisk despite privatization of the hotel industry. The Romanian government has stepped up efforts to promote foreign tourism, including advertising campaigns and tourism promotion abroad. After declining to US$400 million in 2003, tourism revenue has increased sharply, reaching US$1.3 billion in 2005. A program of diversification and intensified promotion aims to double that figure by 2008.

Retail sales have expanded rapidly beginning in 2004, with the expanded presence of large foreign retail companies in the larger cities. In 2005 retail sales increased by 17.6 percent, although the sector still was dominated by small stores and sales volume trailed those in the Czech Republic and Hungary.

Labor: The collapse of the Ceauşescu regime prompted a series of dramatic changes in both the size and composition of the labor force in Romania, which contains a large stock of skilled individuals. The most significant shifts took place in industry, which employed just 2 million Romanians in 2001 after having employed 4 million in 1989. During the 1990s, employment in the gray market increased significantly, complicating efforts to assess the condition of the labor market. In 2005 the labor force was estimated at 9.3 million workers, or some 42 percent of the population. According to estimates in 2004, nearly 3 million Romanians worked in industry and commerce, 2.8 million in services, and 2.4 million in agriculture. Unemployment peaked in 1999 at 11.8 percent. Registered unemployment for 2005 was 5.9 percent, one of the lowest regional official unemployment rates. Unemployment is distributed unevenly, however; it is lowest in Bucharest and the areas closest to the border with Hungary. Many observers believe that the unemployment rate is kept unrealistically low in part by the significant migration of Romanians abroad in search of employment. As of January 2006, the minimum wage was about US$124 per month after being raised from its 2005 level of US$98 per month.

Foreign Economic Relations: In the early years of the postcommunist era, Romania lost most of its trading partners from the former communist bloc, and it also suffered from international sanctions against traditional export markets such as Iraq and the former Yugoslavia. Romania felt the need to regularize and expand its commercial relations to overcome these losses and the eccentric foreign trade policy of the Ceauşescu regime. In 1993 the Romanian government signed a free-trade agreement with the European Free Trade Association, and in 1995 Romania joined the World Trade Organization. Romania is scheduled to join the European Union (EU) in January 2007, a move that will accelerate the existing concentration of its trade relations in Western Europe. Throughout the early 2000s, the EU was Romania's largest market for exports and largest provider of imports. Between 2004 and 2005, trade with Germany increased by 14 percent, and an increase of more than 25 percent occurred in 2006. The Romanian government is working to improve trade relations with neighboring Black Sea states and has championed the creation of a free-trade area for manufactured goods with Bulgaria and Turkey.

Imports: In 2004 the total value of imports was US$32.7 billion; in 2005 the total increased to US$38.2 billion. In 2001 goods from Italy, Germany, Russia, and France accounted for about 49 percent of all imports. By 2005 that percentage had decreased to 44.5 percent, although those four countries remained Romania's largest suppliers, in the same order of value. Principal imports included machinery and equipment, textiles, petroleum and petroleum products, and chemicals and related products.

Exports: In 2004 export values totaled US$23.5 billion, and in 2005 the total increased to US$27.7 billion. More than 40 percent of all exports went to Italy, Germany, and France, but market diversification in the early 2000s reduced the figure from its 2001 level of nearly 50 percent. Romania's range of exports has remained small because industrial restructuring has been slow. Major exports included textiles, metals, machinery, automobiles, and minerals and fuels.

Trade Balance: Romania has had a persistent trade imbalance, incurring deficits that grew from US$6.4 billion in 2003 to US$9.2 billion in 2005. For the first eight months of 2006, the estimated deficit was US$5.9 billion. Government planning aimed at establishing a trade surplus by 2007 or 2008.

Balance of Payments: Romania ran a current account deficit throughout the 1990s and the early 2000s. Between 2001 and 2005, the deficit increased from US$1.4 billion to US$8.5 billion. Between 1999 and 2004, however, the overall balance of payments has been positive. In 2004 the overall balance of payments was US$6.2 billion.

External Debt: In 2005 Romania's external debt was US$14.7 billion, compared with US$15.6 billion in 2002. The bulk of Romania's external debt was medium- and long-term debt.

Foreign Investment: Although the potential for foreign direct investment (FDI) in Romania is high, the level of FDI has lagged behind other economies in the region. Cumulative FDI between 1989 and 2002 reached US$9 billion, whereas during the same time period in Hungary, cumulative FDI amounted to US$22.5 billion. In 2004 and 2005, FDI increased substantially, reaching US$6.5 billion in the latter year. In the first eight months of 2006, FDI increased by nearly 60 percent compared with the same period of 2005. Some 50 percent of FDI has been targeted to privatization. Although Romania's industries are heavily dependent on FDI, in recent years the greatest FDI growth has occurred in the non-industrial sectors. In recent years, foreign investment has diversified, although Romania still trails other countries in its region in that respect. Large foreign food retailers from France, Germany, and the United Kingdom have expanded their operations rapidly in Romania, and IKEA of Sweden was to begin retailing housewares in 2007. Expansion of the Cernavoda nuclear plant is a joint venture between Atomic Energy of Canada and Ansaldo of Italy. Beginning in the 1990s, major U.S. and European hotel chains have invested heavily in Romania. Renault of France owns the Dacia automotive company, which produces 80 percent of Romania's vehicle output. Alcatel of France helped the state-owned CFR rail company to build a computerized railroad station in Timişoara, and communications companies in Canada, France, and Greece supply mobile telephone services.

Currency and Exchange Rate: Romania's currency is the leu (pl., lei); 100 bani (sing., ban) equal one leu. On July 1, 2005, Romania redenominated its currency; a new (or heavy) leu is valued at 10,000 old lei. At the time of redenomination, the leu was one of the least valued currencies in the world at 29,891 per US$1. As of December 2006, US$1 equaled 2.58 new lei.

Fiscal Year: Calendar year.

TRANSPORTATION AND TELECOMMUNICATIONS

Overview: Development of transportation infrastructure was a low priority under the Ceauşescu regime. As a result, in the early 2000s Romania's road and rail systems have remained among the least extensive in Europe, and the networks' state of disrepair continues to hamper commercial connections with the rest of Europe and foreign investment. Plans call for improving and linking the transportation infrastructure with trans-European transport networks. Transport modernization is a high government priority, as well as a key component of European Union (EU) accession negotiations. The cost of upgrading roads between 2004 and 2007 is estimated at US$3.3 billion, part of which will be funded by the EU.

Roads: In 2003 Romania had 60,000 kilometers of paved roads, 228 kilometers of which were rated as expressways. Significant portions of this system are in poor condition, and 46 percent of public roads are located in rural areas. Among projects for the near future are a new highway from Bucharest to Constanţa as part of the Pan-European Corridor IV project and a ring road around Bucharest. Corridor IV would link Dresden with Istanbul and Thessaloniki via Romania. Romania has received significant funding from several European lenders for road infrastructure improvements.

Railroads: Rail is the major form of domestic transportation in Romania; the rail network includes 10,898 kilometers of standard-gauge rail line. However, only 35 percent of this network is electrified, and capital equipment and infrastructure require updating. In 2005 the rail network carried about 500,000 passengers per day and 70 million tons of freight for the year. In 2005 railroad stations with computerized routing systems were operating in four major cities. A modernized rail connection between Bucharest and Constanţa will make possible train speeds of up to 160 kilometers per hour.

Ports: Romania has ports on the Black Sea and along the Danube River; most are in need of repair and modernization. Constanţa, Romania's principal oil port, covers nearly 4,000 hectares on the Black Sea and has an annual handling capacity of 115 million tons. North of Constanţa, a satellite port, Midia, handles 200,000 tons of cargo annually. Danube River ports are vital to Romania because the river is its main commercial link with Central Europe. The main port along the Danube River is Galaţi, which handles approximately 6.7 million tons of cargo annually. In descending order of annual cargo volume, other ports along the Danube are Tulcea, Giurgiu, Orşova, Medgidia, Zimnicea, Turnu Măgurele, Olteniţa, and Sulina.

Inland Waterways: The Danube is by far Romania's most important river for transportation. The Danube is an important route for domestic shipping as well as international trade. It is navigable for river vessels along its entire Romanian course and for seagoing ships as far as the port of Braila, about 150 kilometers inland. Problems with reliance on the Danube for inland transportation are its remoteness from most major industrial centers and marshy banks and flooding that impede navigation in some areas. The Danube–Black Sea Canal provides an east-west shortcut from Constanţa to the meandering lower Danube. Plans call for extensive new commercial development along the canal.

Civil Aviation and Airports: In 2006 Romania had 61 airports, 25 of which had permanently surfaced runways. Of these, seven are classified as international. Bucharest International Airport at Otopeni is the largest in the country, carrying some 3 million passengers and 25,000 tons of cargo per year. The other airports served by international flights are Cluj-Napoca, Constanţa, Targu-Mures, Sibiu, Arad, Oradea, and Timişoara. The government's master plan for airport development through the year 2015 calls for modernization of all major airports, including runway lengthening and widening, improved safety, and possible privatization. Early targets of that program have been the facilities at Cluj-Napoca and Bucharest. Efforts to privatize the national airline, Tarom Romanian Airlines, have suffered frequent postponements. Tarom's small fleet now includes mainly new Western aircraft. Plans called for passenger volume to increase from 1.45 million in 2006 to 1.8 million in 2008. Membership in the European Union will substantially increase Tarom's competition.

Pipelines: Two state-owned companies control Romania's network of approximately 2,400 kilometers of petroleum pipelines. The first, Petrotrans, carries crude oil from the Black Sea port of Constanţa to refineries inland; and the second, owned by Conpet, carries crude oil from oil fields in the south and east to refineries in Cîmpina, Dărmăneşti, Oneşti, and Ploieşti. In addition, Romania has approximately 3,500 kilometers of natural gas pipelines that bring gas into Romania from Bulgaria, Greece, and Russia (via Ukraine). The proposed Southeast European Pipeline, one Romanian segment of which already exists, would bring oil from the Black Sea across Romania to Italy's Adriatic port of Trieste. Negotiations were ongoing in late 2006. The Nabucco Pipeline would connect West European natural gas users with the transcaspian line, crossing Romania and several other countries to reach Germany. Final negotiations were held in 2006, and construction could be completed in 2010.

Telecommunications: After deregulation, expansion, and modernization over the past 10 years, Romania's telecommunications sector has grown rapidly since 2003, particularly in information technology (IT). In 2006 Romania had the highest per capita ratio of IT specialists in Europe. The market for mobile phone services in Romania is one of the most advanced in the Balkans, with mobile service more widely used than fixed-line. Of the four mobile service providers, three are foreign companies. In 2006 Romania had 14.9 million mobile service subscribers (compared with 10.2 million in 2004); the number of landlines remained stable at about 4.5 million. Internet penetration is weak by European standards, but access has increased rapidly since the early 2000s. By 2005 Romania had an estimated 4.9 million Internet users (compared with 158,000 in 1998) and 56,200 Internet hosts. Online journalism increased significantly in 2005, albeit from a modest starting point.

GOVERNMENT AND POLITICS

Overview: Romania is a republic with a directly elected president and a bicameral legislature. In the postcommunist era, Romania generally has had a democratic system of government, although until 2004 governance was dominated by a single figure, Ion Iliescu (who has been elected president three times), and parties associated with him. The European Union (EU) has identified reform of Romania's public administration as a requirement for membership. After the Ceauşescu regime fell in 1989, a new constitution was ratified in 1991. It was last modified by referendum in October 2003.

Executive Branch: The executive branch is composed of the president (head of state), the prime minister (head of government), and the Council of Ministers (cabinet). The president is elected by popular vote and cannot serve more than two five-year terms (extended by a constitutional referendum from four years in 2003). The president serves as supreme commander of the armed forces, chairs the Supreme Defense Council, and nominates the prime minister. The prime minister, who was Calin Popescu-Tariceanu in 2006, appoints the government (Council of Ministers), which must be confirmed by a vote of confidence from parliament. In 2006 the government included 15 ministries, three deputy prime ministers, and the head of the National Bank of Romania; some reorganization was expected following admission to the European Union (EU) in 2007.

Legislature: The legislative branch, a two-chamber parliament, is made up of the Chamber of Deputies (Camera Deputatilor, 332 seats) and the Senate (Senat, 137 seats); all seats are filled by popular vote. Deputies and senators serve four-year terms. As at the lower levels of government, all seats in the national parliament are allocated in proportion to the votes gained by the parties. The legislature has been weakened by the availability of an "emergency ordinance" strategy that enables the executive branch to pass legislation without parliamentary approval. However, in recent years European Union law has been the model for a substantial portion of Romania's new legislation.

The parliamentary elections of 2004 gave the Social Democratic Party (SDP) a plurality of seats in the Chamber of Deputies, but a coalition of three parties, the Justice and Truth Alliance (DA), the Hungarian Democratic Union in Romania (HDUR), and the Romanian Humanist Party (PUR), formed a government based on their combined numbers. Between 2004 and late 2006, some deputies changed party allegiance, giving the DA (itself an alliance of the National Liberal Party and the Democratic Party) an independent plurality. As of October 2006, the party alignment of the Chamber of Deputies was as follows: DA, 118; SDP, 105; the Greater Romania Party (GRP), 31; HDUR, 22; Conservative Party (formerly the PUR), 18; other parties, 18; and independents, 19. The distribution in the Senate was as follows: DA, 50; SDP, 43; GRP, 18; Conservatives, 11; HDUR, 10; and independents, 11. The president of the Chamber of Deputies, Bogdan Olteanu, was elected in March 2006 when the previous president, former prime minister Adrian Năstase, was forced to resign because of alleged corruption.

Judiciary: The judicial branch is divided into a Constitutional Court, a lower court system with municipal and county courts, a court of appeals, and a High Court of Cassation and Justice. The role of the High Court of Cassation and Justice, as defined by the constitution, is to ensure a unitary and consistent interpretation and enforcement of the law by all lower courts. The nine-member Constitutional Court addresses the constitutionality of challenged laws and decrees. The members serve nonconcurrent nine-year terms. The two houses of parliament and the president appoint three judges each to the Constitutional Court. Judges to the High Court of Cassation and Justice serve six-year terms and may serve multiple terms; like all other judges in the lower court system, they are appointed by the president on the recommendation of the 19-member Superior Council of Magistrates. The constitution provides for an independent judiciary; judges appointed by the president cannot be removed prior to the end of their terms.

Administrative Divisions: Romania is divided into 41 counties (*judete*; sing., *judet*). Below the county level are three categories of population centers: 2,800 communes, having fewer than 5,000 inhabitants; 280 towns, having 5,000 to 20,000 inhabitants; and 86 municipalities, having more than 20,000 inhabitants.

Provincial and Local Government: Each of Romania's 41 counties is governed by a county council, whose members are elected by party; municipalities, towns, and communes are administered by mayors (elected individually) and local councils (elected by party). The county council coordinates the actions of all commune and town councils within a given county. Each county and Bucharest has a prefect appointed by the central government, who is charged with representing the central government at the local level. The prefect can block the actions of a local authority under certain conditions, such as violations of the law or the constitution. Such contested matters are then referred to an administrative court for arbitration. Reform proposals by President Traian Basescu in 2006 would give municipalities and county councils substantially greater responsibility for education, health care, and police services now provided by the central government. The inefficient county administrative system may be replaced by a regional system after 2007, but this controversial reform will await Romania's entry into the European Union.

Judicial and Legal System: The Romanian legal system is based on the Napoleonic Code. The law does not provide for jury trials; therefore, judges alone decide the outcome of trials. The law stipulates the right to counsel and presumption of innocence until proven guilty. The system has three levels below the High Court of Cassation and Justice: a lower court, an intermediate court, and an appellate court. Courts at each level have a prosecutor's office. In the early 2000s, the Romanian legal system struggled to cope with a steadily increasing volume of court cases, particularly commercial litigation, and a shortage of judges. In 2004 and 2005, reports by the European Commission criticized the Romanian judiciary for lack of political independence and training and for unfamiliarity with the law of the European Union (EU). A judicial reform law passed in 2005 aimed at increasing the independence and professionalism of judges and prosecutors. Minister of Justice Monica Macovei, a nonpolitical appointee, has received credit for accelerating the judicial reform process, a major factor in the EU's final approval of Romania's membership in 2006. The 2006 state budget increased funding of the judicial branch by 12 percent.

Electoral System: Representatives to the two houses of parliament are chosen by direct, popular vote on a proportional representation basis for four-year terms. Parliamentary elections last were held on November 28, 2004, when 58 percent of eligible voters cast ballots. The organization and conduct of national elections are the responsibility of the Central Election Bureau, which has branch offices in each county. The Permanent Electoral Authority, created in 2006, monitors the funding of political parties. The next parliamentary elections are scheduled for November 28, 2008.

The president is elected by direct popular vote. The most recent presidential election, held on November 28, 2004, resulted in a runoff between the top two candidates on December 12, 2004. In that election, Traian Basescu of the Democratic Party defeated incumbent prime minister Adrian Năstase of the Social Democratic Party with 51.2 percent of the vote. The next presidential election will be held on November 28, 2009, with a runoff on December 12, 2009, if necessary.

Politics and Political Parties: As of 2006, political parties represented in parliament include the National Liberal Party (NLP) and the Democratic Party (DP), which together formed the Justice and Truth Alliance (DA); the Hungarian Democratic Union in Romania (HDUR); the Conservative Party; the Social Democratic Party (SDP); and the ultranationalist Greater Romania Party. In 2006 the main parties of the governing coalition, the center-right NLP and the center-left DP, were increasingly hostile and not expected to remain partners in the Justice and Truth Alliance for the next election (in 2007 or 2008). The SDP, which had suffered serious scandals, was not expected to be a serious factor, and the NLP was weakened by factionalism. A new coalition was expected to head the next government. Parties failing to gain seats in parliament in the 2004 elections include the National Peasant and Christian-Democrat Party (PNTCD), the Popular Action Party (AP), the New Generation Party (PNG), the Union for Romania's Reconstruction (URR), and the Democrat Force (FD).

Mass Media: The fall of the Ceauşescu regime brought extensive changes in Romanian media markets. In 2006 the mass media market remained a balance between state-owned and independent outlets. In the 2004 presidential election, international monitors criticized the broadcast media for favoritism but found the print media basically fair. Although 2005 saw a significant increase in the unimpeded reporting of controversial views, the state continued to use advertising revenue and other devices to influence coverage in the broadcast media. Financial restraints on media freedom are particularly pronounced in the provinces. In 2005 two national and several other state-owned television channels and four state-owned national radio stations were broadcasting. At least 13 private national channels competed with public television. Some 3.3 million households had cable television, and about 150 FM radio stations were operating. In 2005 Romanians had 12.1 million radios and 11.4 million television sets.

In 2005 Romania had more than 100 newspapers, 18 of which are in Bucharest. The tabloid *Libertatea* had the top circulation of about 200,000 per day; its main competitors included *Jurnalul National*, *Adevarul*, and *Evenementul Zilei*. The early 2000s saw a consolidation of major media groups. By 2004 the Swiss Ringier group owned three of the top-circulation daily newspapers, and the Mediapro group owned the major private television network, several other large stations, and radio and print outlets. The largest domestic news agency is the independent Mediafax. The state-run agency Rompress has received substantial criticism for bias. The major West European news agencies and agencies of Bulgaria, Hungary, Poland, and Russia have offices in Bucharest.

Foreign Relations: Since the demise of the Ceauşescu regime, Romania has actively pursued closer relations with the West and with the United States and the European Union (EU) in particular. Romania is a member of the Organization for Security and Co-operation in Europe (OSCE), joined the North Atlantic Treaty Organization (NATO) in March 2004, and is scheduled to join the EU in 2007. The last hurdle to EU membership was final approval by the European Commission, which occurred in April 2006. Relations with neighbors Bulgaria and Hungary, often tense in the past, have improved significantly since 2000 with the prospect of EU membership. No major issues exist with Serbia, the neighbor to the West. Relations with Russia are on generally cordial terms, although Russia has expressed concern over Romania's membership in NATO and potential accession to the EU. In 2003 Russia and Romania signed a Treaty on Friendly Relations and Cooperation. Although relations with Ukraine have improved in recent years, territory and oil drilling rights at the mouth of the Danube remain in dispute. An eventual goal of Romanian foreign policy is reunification with the neighboring former Soviet republic of Moldova (then Moldavia), which was part of Romania until 1940 and 60 percent of whose population is ethnically Romanian.

Major International Memberships: Romania is a member of the Australia Group, Bank for International Settlements, Black Sea Economic Cooperation Zone, Central European Initiative, Council of Europe, Euro-Atlantic Partnership Council, European Bank for Reconstruction and Development, European Union (applicant), Food and Agriculture Organization, G–9, G–77, International Atomic Energy Agency, International Bank for Reconstruction and Development, International Chamber of Commerce, International Civil Aviation Organization, International Confederation of Free Trade Unions, International Criminal Court, International Criminal Police Organization (Interpol), International Federation of Red Cross and Red Crescent Societies, International Finance Corporation, International Fund for Agricultural Development, International Labour Organization, International Maritime Organization, International Monetary Fund, International Olympic Committee, International Organization for Migration, International Organization for Standardization, International Red Cross and Red Crescent Movement, International Telecommunication Union, Latin American Integration Association, Multilateral Investment Geographic Agency, Nonaligned Movement (guest), Nuclear Suppliers Group, Organisation for the Prohibition of Chemical Weapons, Organization for Security and Co-operation in Europe, Organization of American States (observer), Partnership for Peace, Permanent Court of Arbitration, United Nations, United Nations Conference on Trade and Development, United Nations Educational, Scientific, and Cultural Organization, United Nations Industrial Development Organization, Universal Postal Union, Western European Union (associate affiliate), World Confederation of Labor, World Customs Organization, World Federation of Trade Unions, World Health Organization, World Intellectual Property Organization, World Meteorological Organization, World Tourism Organization, World Trade Organization, and Zangger Committee.

Major International Treaties: Romania is a party to the Chemical Weapons Convention, the Convention on the Prohibition of the Development, Production, and Stockpiling of Bacteriological (Biological) and Toxin Weapons and on Their Destruction, and the Treaty on the Non-Proliferation of Nuclear Weapons. Romania is also a party to the following international environmental agreements: Air Pollution, Air Pollution-Persistent Organic Pollutants, Antarctic Treaty, Biodiversity, Climate Change, Climate Change–Kyoto Protocol, Desertification,

Endangered Species, Environmental Modification, Hazardous Wastes, Law of the Sea, Ozone Layer Protection, Ship Pollution, and Wetlands.

NATIONAL SECURITY

Armed Forces Overview: Romania has 97,200 military personnel, organized in the army (66,000, including 18,500 conscripts), navy (7,200), and air force (14,000, including 3,800 conscripts), as well as some units under joint command (10,000). In preparation for accession to the European Union (EU) in 2007, Romania's military is undertaking changes to bring it in line with EU standards for member states. In addition, in order to join the North Atlantic Treaty Organization (which it did in 2004), Romania committed to a minimum expenditure of 2 percent of gross domestic product on defense spending. Nonetheless, Romania's military currently is constrained by outdated equipment and national budget limitations.

Foreign Military Relations: The United States began training the Romanian military through the International Military Education and Training program in 1993. Since the early 2000s, Romania has focused on establishing effective cooperation with the military organizations of the other North Atlantic Treaty Organization (NATO) countries. To reinforce the new Central European region of the alliance, Romania has sought closer strategic relationships with Hungary and Poland. Romania has offered diplomatic advice for political conflict resolution as well as troops for NATO's Kosovo Force, in order to advance the critical goal of stability in neighboring former Yugoslavia. To bring its air force closer to NATO standards, Romania has received technical assistance from Israel and has sought secondhand aircraft from NATO allies in Europe.

External Threat: Romania faces no threat of conventional armed conflict.

Defense Budget: Defense spending in Romania declined significantly after the fall of the Ceauşescu regime in 1989, but spending has grown as a percentage of gross domestic product since 2000. In 2005 the defense budget was US$1.96 billion. The 2006 budget allotted US$2.13 billion, and the projected budget for 2007 was US$2.8 billion.

Major Military Units: The Romanian army has one joint operations command (corps), two operations commands (divisions), one land forces headquarters, and two territorial corps commands with 10 active brigades (one tank, three mechanized, one mountain, one airborne, one artillery, one antiaircraft, one engineering, and one logistical) and 14 territorial brigades (one tank, six mechanized, two mountain, two artillery, two antiaircraft, and one engineering). The navy has a naval headquarters with one naval operational command (fleet level) and one Danube-based riverine flotilla. The air force has a headquarters with one air operational command, one air division, six air bases, and one training base. Plans call for the establishment in 2007 of two new ground force units—one brigade of mountain troops and one infantry brigade—to contribute to the North Atlantic Treaty Organization and European Union combat forces.

Major Military Equipment: According to some estimates, more than half of Romania's military hardware is more than two decades old. Budget constraints make a rapid upgrade of military equipment to Western standards unlikely. In 2006 the Romanian army had 1,258 main battle tanks, 84 assault guns, 4 reconnaissance vehicles, 177 armored infantry fighting vehicles, 1,583 armored personnel carriers, 1,238 pieces of artillery, 9 surface-to-surface missile launchers, 127 antitank missiles, 933 antitank guns, 663 air defense guns, 64 surface-to-air missiles, 10 surveillance vehicles, and 6 unmanned aerial vehicles. The navy had 7 principal surface combatants (3 frigates and 4 corvettes); 3 missile craft; 12 torpedo boats; 38 patrol craft; 1 minelayer; 10 mine countermeasure craft; and 10 logistics and support craft. The air force had 68 MiG–21A and 25 MiG—1C combat aircraft, 11 transport aircraft, 83 training aircraft, 114 utility and support helicopters, 8 assault helicopters, and 42 surface-to-air missiles.

Military Service: In 2006 Romania required eight months of military service for males. Compulsory service begins at 20 years of age; volunteers may enter the service at 18 years of age. Conscription is scheduled to end in 2007.

Paramilitary Forces: In 2006 Romania had a paramilitary force of 79,900 under the control of the Ministry of Interior. Of that number, 22,900 were border guards, and about 57,000 were in the gendarmerie. Because of Romania's location at the eastern frontier of the European Union (EU), reforming and streamlining the Border Police was a high priority in advance of its admittance to the EU.

Military Forces Abroad: In 2006 Romania had 400 soldiers serving as part of the U.S. mission in Afghanistan and 550 troops with the North Atlantic Treaty Organization's International Security Assistance Force in Afghanistan, as well as one mechanized infantry brigade of 860 troops in Iraq. In addition, Romanian troops participate in the following United Nations missions: Afghanistan (550), Bosnia (120), Côte d'Ivoire (5 observers) Democratic Republic of Congo (22 observers), Ethiopia/Eritrea (7 observers), and the Kosovo Force (KFOR; 308).

Foreign Military Forces: In June 2006, Romania's parliament ratified a controversial bilateral agreement that would allow a U.S. military presence at several bases in eastern Romania. Bulgarian, Romanian, and U.S. forces conducted joint ground forces exercises on Romanian territory in summer 2006.

Police: Romania's police are divided into two organizations, both of which fall under the jurisdiction of the Ministry of Interior: the gendarmerie and the national police, which is the main civil law enforcement agency. Each of the 41 counties has its own police organization under the overall control of the general inspectorate. The general inspectorate investigates crimes of national significance such as organized crime and economic and financial malfeasance. A program of reorganization and modernization, begun in 2004 to meet European Union standards, will divide the force into departments for organized crime prevention, criminal investigations, and public order and safety, and administration is to be decentralized. The gendarmerie, a police force with military status, is responsible for crowd and riot control, patrolling mountainous and coastal areas, apprehending fugitives and deserters, counterterrorism operations, and guarding sensitive installations such as the nuclear power plant, embassies, and international airports. Like the national police, it is divided into 41 county jurisdictions. The gendarmerie's special intervention brigade handles national incidents of terrorism, hostage-taking, and heavy rioting.

Internal Threat and Terrorism: Although post-Ceauşescu Romania has had periods of civil unrest (often related to disputes over political reforms and budget cuts), there is no evidence of terrorism or other internal threats.

Human Rights: The Romanian government generally respects the civil liberties of citizens, although police abuses continue to be reported. In addition, in 2006 a report by the European Commission stated that further measures are required to guarantee the political independence and professionalism of judges and prosecutors. Reports of police brutality continued in 2005, as did allegations of the failure of the government to fully prosecute such cases. The government also has been accused at times of restricting freedom of the press. Journalists who wrote reports critical of government policies and actions have claimed they were targets of harassment and intimidation, although such incidents have decreased under the government formed in 2004. Religious minorities have complained of discriminatory treatment by the government. Societal harassment of ethnic and sexual minorities remains a problem, as do violence and discrimination against women. Major cities continue to have large populations of homeless children. In the early 2000s, the government began to address the chronic problem of trafficking in females for the purposes of prostitution. Discrimination and violence against the Roma minority remain widespread, as the government has not punished such discrimination consistently. Child labor abuses have been reported, as well as government interference in trade union activities.